DAYS OF TRAGEDY

The Killing of a Rock Legend:
JOHN LENNON

Written by:
Sue L. Hamilton

1

Published by Abdo & Daughters, 6537 Cecilia Circle, Bloomington, Minnesota 55435

Library bound edition distributed by Rockbottom Books, Pentagon Tower, P.O. Box 36036, Minneapolis, Minnesota 55435

Library of Congress Number: 89-084907   ISBN: 0-939179-59-8

Cover Photo by: Michael Ochs Archive
Inside Photos by: Bettmann Newsphotos and Michael Ochs Archive

Edited by: John C. Hamilton

FORWARD

December 8, 1980. 10:50 p.m.

A cool glow flowed from the street lights outside New York's Dakota, a huge old building where rock legend John Lennon and his wife, Yoko Ono, owned five apartments. Out front, a 25-year-old man waited in the shadows. It wasn't unusual. The Lennons were often asked to sign their autographs, which they were happy to do.

Returning from a five-hour session at their recording studio, the Lennon's car drove up to the front of the apartment building. Just as he did on any other night, José the doorman opened the limo's door. John stepped out into the night air. It was warm for December. He took a few steps, with Yoko close behind. From the shadows, a voice called out to him, "Mr. Lennon?"

John started to turn when suddenly the blasts of a .38 revolver froze his movements. Five shots hit the 5'11" rock star square in the back. Blood flowed freely as he staggered up the Dakota's steps, moaning, "I'm shot! I'm shot!"

Lurching into an inside office, he fell to the floor. Jay Hastings, another doorman, saw his favorite tenant covered with blood. Hastings quickly pressed the alarm button to bring the police. Minutes later, sirens blaring, the cars arrived. John Lennon was rushed to nearby Roosevelt Hospital. But the man who pleaded in song to "Give Peace A Chance" was dead. At age 40, the ex-Beatle, father, husband, song writer, musician, and artist lost his life to the violent madness of a lone gunner: a fan.

John Lennon.

CHAPTER 1 — A TOUGH BOYHOOD

On October 9, 1940, at 6:30 p.m. , amidst the screams of air raid sirens and German bombs of World War II, John Winston Lennon was born in Liverpool, England. His mother, Julia, watched as he was wrapped up warmly in a blanket, and tucked underneath her bed for safety. His father, Alfred, who worked on board ships, was away at sea, but Mary Elizabeth Smith, his mother's sister (who he came to call Aunt Mimi), risked a trip through the dangerous streets to have a look at him. "He's beautiful!" said Aunt Mimi. Julia agreed.

John's father was often at sea, spending months away from his family. Julia, a fun-loving and carefree woman, found that raising a baby alone was not easy. Within months after his birth, John was staying with Aunt Mimi and her husband, Uncle George, and by age two he was living with them full time.

Aunt Mimi quickly realized that John Lennon was not going to be an easy boy to care for. From his earliest days, John wanted to do things his own way, to be in charge. He grew into a bully and was often in trouble at school. He would tease others, especially if there was something wrong with them physically. John himself was very near-sighted, and at first refused to wear glasses. He feared that they would make him look weak, something he hated. Aunt Mimi insisted, but it wasn't until she agreed to buy him special horn-rimmed glasses, like the ones his idol, rock star Buddy Holly, wore, that John would get them. Even then, he only wore them when he had to.

With John often in trouble, Aunt Mimi tried to be very strict with him. She insisted he attend school and wear the proper clothes, although John would often arrive late with his tie crooked and the top button of his shirt undone. While Aunt Mimi struggled to keep him in line, John turned to Uncle George for a few bends in the rules. Uncle George was kind, often taking John to his dairy to watch the cows being milked or sneaking him a treat when John was in trouble with Aunt Mimi.

In September 1952, John graduated from Dovedale Primary School and went on to Quarry Bank High School. While he still insisted on doing things his own way, several teachers saw that he did well in art and encouraged him. Life moved on for the young teenager. Although still a rebel, things seemed to be going OK, until June 5, 1955, when Uncle George died. John was deeply hurt by the sudden death of his kindly uncle. It was the first of several tragic deaths that John would have to deal with.

During this time, John began seeing more of his mother. She played banjo and taught John a few chords. It wasn't long before John had his own instrument — a guitar — and was playing as well. In May 1957, at the age of 16, John started his own singing group: the Quarry Men, named after his high school. Although he went to the Liverpool College of Art, from that point on, music would be his life.

CHAPTER 2 — THE BEATLES

On July 6, 1957, the Quarry Men were playing a concert. A 15-year-old boy saw the concert and asked a friend to introduce him to the leader of the group. Paul McCartney met John Lennon, and John quickly discovered that Paul, a much more experienced guitar player, would really help him and the group. Paul was invited to join. He accepted, although he would have to wait a couple months until he got back from scout camp.

Seven months later, 15-year-old George Harrison, also an excellent guitarist, was asked to join the group. There would be several drummers in the band until August 1962, when Ringo Starr took the job, but the center of a rock n' roll legend had formed by early 1958.

At Aunt Mimi's insistence, John remained at the College of Art, where he met Cynthia Powell (his future wife) and Stuart Sutcliffe (his best friend). John's world centered on his music. It would help him to deal with his next tragedy. After visiting Aunt Mimi on July 15, 1958, John's mother was crossing the road headed for a bus stop, when a car struck and killed her. She died instantly. It

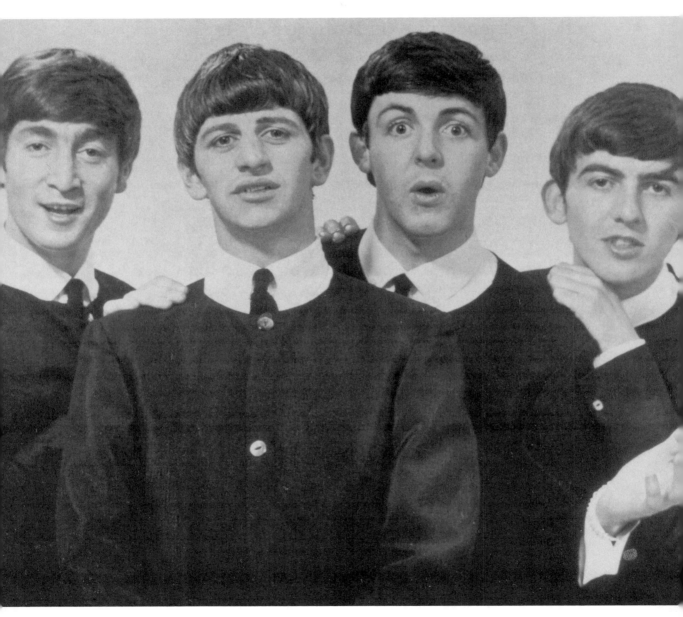

The Beatles in the early 60s. From left to right: John Lennon, Ringo Starr, Paul McCartney and George Harrison.

was a painful time for the 17-year-old John, but he kept on with his work.

John often convinced Paul, who attended the Liverpool Institute next door to the College of Art, to skip out of school and spend an afternoon writing songs. With John's new ideas and Paul's gift for detail, they were a great team.

As times changed, so changed the group's name. The Quarry Men became Johnny and the Moon Dogs in 1959. That still wasn't right. Buddy Holly, whose music John and Paul both loved, had a backup group called "The Crickets." It was John's best friend, Stuart, who came up with a similar name, "The Beetles." John liked that, but added his own flair by changing the spelling and using the word "beat." Thus was born, "The Beatles."

Their rise to fame was one of the quickest in music history. In 1962, now with Ringo Starr as drummer, The Beatles' manager, Brian Epstein, got a record contract with E.M.I. Records. Sadly, Stuart never lived to see the group he had help name reach the top. He died in April, one month before the contract was signed.

Lennon in later years, at the end of the Beatles career.

However, nothing could stop the popularity of this new English group. By 1963, "Please Please Me" was a number one hit. Soon, every new song they released went to the top of the music charts. They held concerts worldwide, and with their popularity came T.V. appearences, movies, and magazine interviews. The Beatles were rich and famous, but there was a price. Drugs and alcohol became a major part of their lives. The screams of the crowd were so loud, their music went almost unheard. What had started out as fun had turned into a job — and one that none of the four enjoyed. On August 29, 1966, after three years of concert touring, The Beatles gave their last live performance at Candlestick Park in San Francisco. Less then three months later, John would meet an artist that would change his life forever.

John Lennon and Yoko Ono were married on March 20, 1969.

CHAPTER 3 — JOHN AND YOKO

On November 9, 1966, John went to a London art show. There he saw strange paintings and sculptures done by a dark-haired Japanese woman, Yoko Ono. Although John at first referred to her as "that weird artist woman," he soon found her ideas interesting and much like his own. However, both John and Yoko were married.

Lennon's wife of four years, Cynthia, had stayed quietly in the shadows of her husband's popularity. When their son, John Charles Julian Lennon was born on April 8, 1963, Cynthia was happy to stay at home, being a part-time wife to John and full-time mother to Julian. Cynthia hadn't changed even through all the ups and downs of Beatlemania, but John had. Later, even Cynthia would admit that Yoko was the right one for John.

By March 20, 1969, having each divorced their previous mates, John and Yoko were married. The next 11 years would be years of learning and peace for John Lennon. The Beatles dissolved, never to get back together again. Except for a

John with his son Julian, from his first marriage to Cynthia Powell.

fight that separated them for 14 months between 1973 and 1975, John and Yoko were together almost constantly. They waged a war for peace, singing and holding demonstrations. "Give Peace A Chance" was their first song recorded together. In December 1969, they put up huge posters and billboards in 11 cities around the world which read, "War Is Over! If You Want It. Happy Christmas from John and Yoko."

They settled in New York in an apartment in a large old building known as the Dakota. As John said, "It's so safe here. I feel free, walking the streets. Nobody hassles you." For several years he was right.

On October 9, 1975, John's 35th birthday, Sean Taro Ono Lennon was born. For the next five years, John took the roll of househusband, raising Sean. In August 1980, he and Yoko began recording their first album. Released as *Double Fantasy* on November 17, 1980, John Lennon was back on the music scene, but sadly, not for long.

CHAPTER 4 — THE KILLER

Mark David Chapman was born in Ft. Worth, Texas, in 1955. His family moved to Atlanta, Georgia, where Chapman grew up. Chapman and his best friend, Garry Limuti, loved the Beatles. True fans, they bought guitars and spent hours listening to Beatles songs and trying to play them. Chapman's room was covered with posters and photographs of the "Fab Four," and Chapman kept his hair in the trendy Beatles moptop. Although they loved the group, both boys agreed that John Lennon was their favorite Beatle.

Chapman, not unlike many teens of the '60s, began to experiment with drugs. He took LSD, and had several "bad trips." Confused and frightened, Chapman ran away from home for short periods of time. But at age 15, he did a complete turnaround. He turned from drugs and Beatlemania to religion and God. He cut his hair and began wearing a tie and carrying a Bible. However, in 1966, after an interview where John Lennon had said that the Beatles were more popular than Jesus, Chapman was furious. Many people in Chapman's prayer group, and people

Mark David Chapman; the man who killed John Lennon.

across the nation, were equally angry with these young men who compared themselves to Jesus. Although Lennon and the rest of the Beatles went on the air to say they were sorry, that it was all a misunderstanding, Chapman still held a grudge against his former idol. His prayer group did a hateful word-play on Lennon's "Imagine" song, singing "Imagine, imagine if John Lennon was dead."

After graduating from high school, Chapman became a YMCA camp counselor, eventually ending up in Fort Chaffee, Arkansas. He worked long hours helping the kids, and did a good job. And Chapman hated guns. "Why do we have so many guns in America?" he asked another YMCA worker, after seeing one in a pickup truck. However, sadly, that view was to change.

After dropping out of a small college in Tennessee, Chapman returned to Atlanta and trained as a security guard at the Atlanta Area Technical School. In order to become a guard, he had to score 60 points on his pistol-firing test. Chapman got an 88. He worked as a guard until early 1977, then moved to Hawaii.

There, he worked in a hospital and with a printer. In 1979, just as Lennon had married an older Japanese woman Yoko Ono, Chapman married Japanese-American Gloria Abe. The two lived in an apartment in Honolulu, which Chapman furnished with expensive paintings, one showing Abraham Lincoln, another victim of an assassin's bullet. Chapman became more and more involved in the art world, taking a lower-paying job as a janitor in a building close to the art galleries. During this time, interest in his teen-age idol once again surfaced. Taping over his own name tag from work, Chapman wrote himself a new name: John Lennon.

From then on, Chapman went downhill. Twice he tried to kill himself, and twice he failed. He was always angry with his wife, and wouldn't let her read newspapers or listen to the radio. At his job, he started a feud with the Church of Scientology across the street. Church members were constantly receiving calls from someone who whispered across the phone lines, "Bang, bang — you're dead." Although they never knew for sure if it was Chapman, the calls stopped about the time Chapman left for New York.

CHAPTER 5 — DEATH OF A ROCK STAR

In October 1980, Chapman quit his job and applied for a gun permit from the Honolulu police. Having no previous criminal record, he was given the permit, and on October 27 bought a five-shot Charter Arms .38 special. He sold one of his paintings to raise some money, and bought a ticket to his home town of Atlanta. He stayed a few days and then returned to Honolulu, but less than a month later, he bought another plane ticket — this time to New York.

On Saturday, December 6, Chapman arrived and got a room at a YMCA only nine blocks from the Dakota, the building where the Lennons lived. Chapman waited outside that day and the following, but it wasn't until early Monday evening that the killer would meet his victim.

It wasn't unusual for people to wait outside the Dakota. The old building was home to many famous people. On Monday, December 8, Chapman waited with another Beatles fan, amateur photographer Paul Goresh. "I've been waiting three days to see Lennon. I want his autograph," said Chapman, holding carefully to his copy of John and Yoko's *Double Fantasy* album. The two waited most of the afternoon, and at about 5:00 p.m. the Lennons walked out.

Chapman timidly walked up and held out the album. John took it and quickly wrote "John Lennon 1980" across the front as Goresh snapped a picture of the fan and his idol. Returning the album, John and Yoko got in their car, headed for a session at The Record Plant Studios.

Chapman watched them drive off. Turning happily to Goresh he exclaimed, "John Lennon signed my album! Nobody in Hawaii is going to believe me."

The two waited together for two more hours, hoping the Lennons would return to sign Goresh's album, but Goresh decided he'd get it another day. He'd waited as long as he wanted to.

"I'd wait," said Chapman seriously, "You never know if you'll see him again." Goresh left, never realizing that this Lennon fan was hinting at the grisly future he had planned for his one-time idol.

At 10:30 p.m. John Lennon arrived back at the Dakota. Crouched in the shadows, both hands on his .38 special, Chapman called "Mr. Lennon?" and emptied his gun into the man who had just 5½ hours earlier autographed his album.

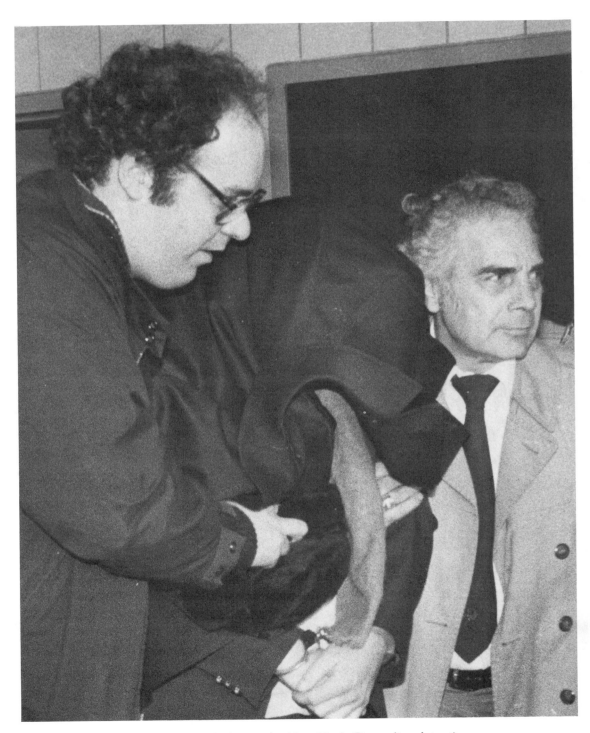

Chapman being led away by New York City police detectives.

CHAPTER 6 — HELLO, GOODBYE

Blood was everywhere as Jay Hastings, the doorman, kicked away the gun that Chapman had dropped to the ground. "Do you know what you just did?" asked a shocked Hastings.

"I just shot John Lennon," said Chapman calmly. Pulling out a copy of the classic novel, "The Catcher in the Rye," Chapman began to thumb through it as he waited for the police to arrive.

Two squad cars, sirens screaming, raced up to the Dakota. Four policemen jumped out, guns drawn. "Put up your hands!" they yelled to Hastings. They mistakenly assumed the wild-eyed and blood-soaked doorman to be the killer.

"Not him," shouted José, the other doorman. "He works here." José pointed at Chapman, calmly reading his book. "He's the one."

Slammed against the Dakota's stone wall, Chapman was quickly arrested. Steps away, just inside the building, lay the young man's victim.

Blood was everywhere. Turning Lennon over, the officer quickly realized they couldn't wait for an ambulance to arrive. With Hastings' help, they carried the broken body of the rock star to their police car and rushed him to the nearest hospital. However, it was too late. Having lost nearly 80% of his blood, the 40-year-old husband, father, and singer died on the way to the hospital. Doctors tried everything to get him back, but John Lennon had said his last goodbye.

John and Yoko, 1980.

EPILOGUE

Alone and frightened, Yoko Ono received the final news from Dr. Stephen Lynn, the hospital's director of emergency services. "We have very bad news," said Lynn. "Unfortunately, in spite of massive efforts, your husband is dead. There was no suffering in the end."

"Are you saying he is sleeping?" sobbed Yoko, unable to believe her husband of nearly 11 years was gone. But as always, Yoko took charge. Returning to the Dakota only an hour and a half after the shooting, she made three phone calls. The first to John's eldest son, Julian, then 17, the same age as when John himself had lost his mother. The next to Aunt Mimi. And finally to Paul McCartney.

By 1:00 a.m. news had spread throughout New York and the world. Crowds formed outside the Dakota, chanting "Give Peace A Chance" and playing Beatles music.

No funeral was held, but Yoko asked for a 10-minute period of silence on Sunday, December 14, at 2:00 p.m. "John loved and prayed for the human race," she said. "Please pray the same for him."

John Lennon - New York City.

Thousands did just that, gathering together to remember and cry for the tragic loss of a rock legend whose music they loved. Aunt Mimi had once told John in his early days as a musician, "The guitar is all right as a hobby, John, but you'll never make a living from it." John did live by it, and tragically, died by it, too.

In the 1965 song "We Can Work It Out," written mostly by Paul McCartney, John added one line: "Life is very short and there's no time for fussing and fighting, my friend." Little did he know how short a time he had left. At age 40, John Lennon died from the cold bullets of a fan's gun. But his music lives on.

SOURCES CONSULTED

Bair, Julia with Giuliano, Geoffrey. **John Lennon, My Brother.** New York: Henry Holt and Company, 1988.

Coleman, Ray. **Lennon.** New York: McGraw-Hill Book Company, 1984.

"Death of a Beatle." **Newsweek,** December 22, 1980.

Graustark, Barbara. "An Ex-Beatle 'Starting Over'." **Newsweek.** December 22, 1980.

Green, John. **Dakota Days.** New York: St. Martin's Press, 1983.

Kroll, Jack. "Strawberry Fields Forever." **Newsweek.** December 22, 1980.

The Editors of Rolling Stone. **The Ballad of John and Yoko.** New York: Doubleday & Company, Inc., 1982.